THE TROUBLE WITH LIGHT

DEDICATION

To those three graces, my nieces, Sally, Sarah and Linda.

ACKNOWLEDGEMENT

Some of the poems in this volume have appeared in: *Canadian Literature*, *The Cormorant*, *The Nashwaak Review*, and *The Prairie Journal of Canadian Literature*.

THE TROUBLE WITH LIGHT

by

Fred Cogswell

Borealis Press
Nepean, Canada
1996

The Publisher gratefully acknowledges the financial support of the Department of Canadian Heritage.

Canadian Cataloguing in Publication Data

Cogswell, Fred, 1917-
  The trouble with light

Poems.
ISBN 0-88887-919-9 (bound) -
ISBN 0-88887-140-6 (pbk.)

    I. Title.

PS8505.048T76 1996   C811'.54   C95-9004-04-1
PR9199.3.C64T76 1996

Published by Borealis Press, Ltd.
9 Ashburn Drive, Nepean, Ontario K2E 6N4

Cover picture by permission Royal Collection Enterprises Ltd.
Artist: VERMEER, Johannes (1632-1675)
Title: A Lady at the Virginals with a Gentleman
Inv/Neg no.: CW 230 WC 109 RCIN 405346
Photographed by Stephen Chapman June 1996

Printed and bound in Canada

CONTENTS

FALL WALK

I still remember what the farm looked like
In the Fall when we were young. We would walk
To the farthest pasture, a one-mile hike,
And on the way we'd hardly ever talk.

Late November, and each night Winter's vice
Grew tighter on what leaves were left to brown.
The water in the lane-ruts turned to ice
That broke and tinkled when our boots came down.

The only warm-colored thing was one spruce
Near the orchard. The apple boughs were bare,
And as we breathed it seemed the smell of juice
Still lingered in the taste of morning air.

Careless we ate the air and drank the light
For the last time before the world turned white.

SENSES

every day I bless
the bridge that senses build to
end our loneliness

you touched me and found
in that pressure two skins joined
make one common ground

when we kissed we both
found a fresh joy in the taste
of another's mouth

when your nose sniffed me
my nostrils sniffed back at you
out of sympathy

when I heard your own
true voice then my own words took
echoes from your tone

and where your gaze burned
there I felt and looked behind
though my back was turned

THE MORE

The more you open up your self to me
The more I find incarnate there in you
A beauty that's its own reality
And needs no other shine to make it true.

THE FIRST STEP

He could have been her father. She could well
Have been his daughter, though in many ways
The two were strange to each other. They both
Intuitively sensed the inner life
In each, long held in, offered guarded, rich
Treasures neither had in part disclosed.

Each one dreaded to open doors long closed.
Lest the other not realize too well
The worth of that inner world and the rich
Dialogue become monologue as always
Seems to happen whenever the deep life
Of one is not quite the deep life of both.

In heart and head she did the work for both
And the high-lights of her childhood disclosed.
With her words, that far-off world flowered to life
As he realized that her vision's spell
Had opened a space that in all its ways
To him was new and beautiful and rich.

But was it new? There flowed in him a rich
Response of memory that linked them both
Together like two joining brooks. The ways
Each had taken had not entirely closed
One truth: roots once watered by the same well
Preserve a unity that lasts for life.

She was young, nearer to the springs of life.
He, though, was old and therefore not so rich.
That the two could understand each other well
Became a blessed miracle to both
As what fear of misunderstanding closed
Grew open to communion in all ways.

In her case, intuition had brave ways
To open up the secrets of her life
That far too long its inner fears kept closed;
In his, a long forgotten seed of rich
Youth returned to flower once more. For both
The first step taken turned extremely well.

It brought epiphanies to both in ways
That neither too well understood, a rich
Life of memories that would not be closed.

AT THE HEART OF THE POEM

After the French of Georges Dor

At the heart of the poem
Illusion tightens reality's knot
At the heart of the poem a secret kingdom
For all who flee the land they cannot live in

At the heart of the poem: MANKIND
In itself undesirable
In all things guilty

At the heart of the poem
The weight of the heart
Alone in every breast

CHOICES

All of us want. Because of need we live.
Take is common, backed by brain, guile, and might;
Give is rare, forced by a sense of others' right.
Only in love can one both take and give.

A WISH

There's so little love
in the world. Let's share all that
we have for a start...

Too old to create
flesh offspring, may our changed selves
be our new children...

LOCATIONS

To Narcissus, joy lay in a mirror's view;
The greatest bliss my heart has ever known
Came not in all those days when I was alone
But in rare moments when I was one of two.

A SUSTAINED EPIPHANY

One evening in August, Gail and I
Drove for miles the long road upriver,
Our eyes on the sky as much as driving
Allowed, following the death of the sun
For two magic hours. Both of us shared
An inimitable concert of light
Which flowed through our bodies, drowning all else
In the ebb and flow of soundless rhythms.

Never in all of either of our lives
Did we so thank God for His gift of eyes
And minds to remember all that glory,
The deeper for both because it was shared.

WHEN COHEN SANG

When Cohen sang, a magic cord
Tied knots inside them. Every word
Brought both of them its rhythmic chime
Til "Dance me to the end of time"
Was oil upon their feelings poured.

The oil exploded. Love was lord.
Their bodies made complete accord,
Annihilating space and time
                    when Cohen sang.

The memory of how they soared
Remains for them a precious hoard,
Still eternal and still sublime.
Truth to them in life's pantomime
Is still the joining that occurred
                    when Cohen sang.

THE TEST

the test
                of an art
is the best
                of the heart
and the strength
and length
                of the mind
                combined
with the pains
and strains
                put in it
                to make things fit
and the skill
that hides these still
                in a new free
                unity
which, experienced whole,
can be called soul

ART-MAKING

To make for the crowd
is to make for rewards that
end when we are paid

To make for our selves
exposes the gap between
achievement and dream

No art is easy:
it's best to make for the sake
of a fine thing made

MUSIC LESSON

To the harp my ear
I turned. In its simple air
every note was clear.

On the harpsichord
many complex sounds occurred
but the notes seemed blurred.

I wanted to know
why harps were neglected so.
Then the piano

joined the harp's pure word
to the richer music poured
from the harpsichord.

Now I, quite content
listen as that instrument
outdoes each parent.

SCULPTOR

He spent his life shaping a perfect statue.
The task was only ended when he was old.
By that time what he had done so well he knew.
He did not even cast it, but broke the mold.

WHO WANTS ...

who wants the straight-lined
perfection of machines in
all that's said and done

should look at nature
where a flawed variety
reigns as primal law...

FORM

The lip that sneers at form for being old
        is out of synch with mine:
Only a strong and well-wrought glass should hold
        creation's finest wine.

A SONNET

A sonnet is an easy poem to write
If you remember that it needs to be
No more than a quadruple harmony
In which grammar, sound, feeling, thought unite
To make, thereby, a new thing—one whose might
Is more than its ingredients, designed
Like music to blend eye, ear, heart, and mind
Into its own crescendo of delight.

Whether you close two thoughts (octave, sestet)
Or open one three times, then nail it shut
With the sharp bang of a final couplet,
In any sonnet you have but to put
Right words in right places at the right times.
And just fourteen of them will do for rhymes.

ANTAEUS

Of ancient warriors strong Antaeus
To me had special worth.
When other heroes leaned on heaven
He drew his strength from earth.

MORNING HYMN

Love, love the coming of the light
And raise your eyes to greet the sun.
What matter that it sets at night?

Go, greet the myriad shapes you sight
That glisten as their colours run.
Love, love the coming of the light.

Keep no watch on time, ignore the flight,
But drink the day til day is done
What matter that it sets at night?

Though you be blind, in grievous plight,
Your skin can feel the warmth begun.
Love, love the coming of the light

And raise your eyes in sheer delight
At God's great gift to every one.
What matter that it sets at night?

Its beams have lent your being might
And lit in you another sun.
Love, love the coming of the light.
What matter that it sets at night?

NOON HYMN

No other time is the sky so blue
As now. The wind has blown it clean.
It shines without a cloud in view

To blur the radiance of its hue
That soars beyond earth's richest green.
No other time is the sky so blue,

No other time its beams break through
To dominate the entire scene.
It shines without a cloud in view

And you will find that shine in you
In cells where never light had been.
No other time is the sky so blue

To penetrate what's always true
And make it also glow: There keen
It shines without a cloud in view.

Life's fragments now, no more askew,
Fuse-melt to form one golden mean.
No other time is the sky so blue.
It shines without a cloud in view.

EVENING HYMN

The light has climaxed, in a glow
Eclipsing how it shone before.
It adds fresh glory to its flow

As if in his old age somehow
A miser squandered all his store.
The light has climaxed in a glow.

Just as the trees of Autumn blow
Rich leaves of gold and bronze galore
It adds fresh glory to its flow.

Inside us now, we sense the throe
That oneness brings; from ebb to flow
The light has climaxed in a glow.

Dissolving difference we go,
One with what we never shared before.
It adds fresh glory to its flow.

More than mind and heart can know
Life burns inside us more and more ...
The light has climaxed in a glow.
It adds fresh glory to its flow.

NIGHT HYMN

The light has fled, the day is gone,
And if there's colour left, it's black.
The world of outside sense is done

As if there never were a sun.
I speak and nothing answers back;
The light has fled, the day is gone..

Where now have speed and motion run
Which shaped the earth that now I lack?
The world of outside sense is done

As if it had not been begun
And what I loved there now I lack.
The light is fled, the day is gone

And I would mourn the vanished sun
If there were no more world to track.
The world of outside sense is done.

In me, twinned, there lives another one.
My mind can re-arrange and pack
The light now fled, the day now gone.
In freedom there the world lives on.

FOUND POEMS: IRREVERENT

Church Notice: Germain Street Baptist Church

Do you want to know what hell is like? Come and hear
the reverend Doctor Vincent at evening service on
Sunday.

Informal Confession

I didn't get hot nuts, padre. She couldn't control
herself long enough for that. . .

Overheard in the Vestry

... I don't know if he was a cannon, but he sure
sounded off like a big gun in that church ...

ON HEARING HEAVY METAL

They work not wisely but too well
      to build their sonic hell.
But one thing's sure. Their playing time
      makes silences sublime.

THE WIZARD

After the French of Pierre Mathieu

Snow's silence paralyses fear
Day disguised as night finds fault with moons
Doubt digs itself in
     and the corn-stalks reel

The future moves around limping
     to the rhythmic roll of drums

Then
     the Wizard of the equinox
          bangs on his outlandish guitar
          and turns up his nose at Spring rain
               in the den of our discomfort

SELVES

"Know thyself," spoke Socrates
In accents Athenese.
"I yam what I yam what I yam,"
Cried Popeye, the sailor-man.

When "To thine own self be true,"
Were words that great Shakespeare said,
Did he mean what's born in you
Or the self that the world made?

PAVAN: THE FIVE SENSES

Smell is the oldest sense. We first begin
To draw from the world its familiar
Ingredients, to our own nature kin,
Avoiding all that our bodies find there
Which grates upon the health we have within.

Soon afterward, taste-buds discover food
And find by trial exactly what they need
To make their bodies grow just as they should.
We find, too, that what is not understood
We should eschew or simply never heed.

We focus eyes to bring the outside in.
Though limited, they form a constant guide
For our minds and flesh as, through thick and thin,
They give us patterns which, when we're inside,
We can adopt and operate with pride.

Instrumental touch is in our own skin,
So close and keen it can dissolve all
Barriers momentarily or thin
The walls of difference til what we call
Truth may depend on the prick of a pin.

The ear, a two-way door, makes brotherhood.
By it we give out all that we can bear
Of music, words, and verse, our soul-food,
Until in time to come the living air
Must vibrate to our soundings everywhere.

Smell is the oldest sense. We first begin.
Soon afterward, taste-buds discover food.
We focus eyes to bring the outside in.
Instrumental touch is in our own skin.
The ear, a two-way door, makes brotherhood.

DUCTLESS GLANDS

Our sun-warmed blood denies its birth
And calls itself a child of earth,
But still it keeps inside its doors
Salt tides that washed Jurassic shores.

Salt is the sperm that lust propels.
Salt, too, are grief's translucent wells,
And salty baths of fear and rage
Proclaim our ocean heritage.

AT MOUNT KATAHDIN IN MAY

I

At Mount Katahdin
true to my daily habits
I woke up early

A bright day in May,
all the trails were snow-covered
and there were no clouds

I'd brought my daughter
to join a group of girl-guides
for the year's first climb

Obeying impulse,
I started up the mountain
on the nearest trail

I noticed the path
my feet made in overshoes,
an elephant's spoor,

much larger than that
when, quite awkwardly at times,
I broke through the crust

When at last I got
higher up than the tree-line
there was no more snow

gray, wind-swept, bare
stones under a clear blue sky,
and the stones were warm

Then I sat right down,
took off foot-wear, shoes, and wrung
out my stockings

'Twas the first ever
my ears heard real silence speak
while my eyes drank space

At last, reluctant,
I got shod again and started
to plod down the slope

II

Meanwhile, the girl-guides
had awakened, dressed, eaten,
and begun their climb

On the trail above
they became increasingly
aware of footsteps

and it dawned on them
that whatever had made them
was up there somewhere

Sooner or later
near the top where trails converge
it and they would meet

But the thoughts they had
of what could have made those tracks
did not comfort them

A bear or giant,
the windigo of folk-lore,
gave the climb suspense,

ended at last when
my daughter cried in relief,
"It's only daddy."

APPEAL TO MEMORY

After the French of Alfred Desrochers

Cross your restless fingers on your breast, close
Your eyes. Let your flesh counterfeit the dead
And feign their slumber without hope or dread.
Scarcely allow the air to blow your nose.

You were nothing. Your life but a vain pose.
The wheat you try to grind is for the strong.
Cross hands. Shut your eyes. Let your body belong
To a salt, mud image; peace, I suppose.

Accept the vacuum that's the dark's non-gleam.
Play at death since nothing lives on today
Of your energy, your pride and your merit.

But build an altar in your subdued heart;
To the arcane gods of your teen-age pray
For what is left of your immortal dream.

WHAT ELSE CAN WE SAY

What else can we say when the game is done
And we've no time to play another one?
When our hearts are left with no life at all
To follow the course of a moving ball
Will it matter whether we lost or won?

Whether we played then for profit or fun
Who will remember? Who scored a winning run
How long will any one ever recall?
                                 What else can we say?

Just to have fielded and batted and run,
To have hoped and battled under the sun
Together with others is to stand tall
Whatever the score, and, when doubters call,
                                 What else can we say?

IN OLD AGE

In old age, the gap between think and do
Widens until the flesh is weary of
The mind's demands and but platonic love
Is the one relationship left for you.

In old age, it is easy to be true,
Technically, although a wild fancy feeds
On the flesh of imaginary deeds,
Drawing no more blood than paper tigers do.

In old age, even your mind-life is bare.
Lacking all the fine delights of touch
The fancy has no power to put on
Substantial faith to preserve illusion.
What matters most is that you no longer care
For those things which, years ago, meant so much.

SENILITY

Tomorrow and tomorrow I must spend
In restoration of my far-off past,
But words and pictures tend to blur and blend
And quite escape my senile brain at last.
My will has gone that used to hold them fast.

In routines different from yesterday
Lie all I have that made my life worthwhile.
I can do nothing on my own. My way
Has no identity. My frown or smile
Can't borrow time, even for a while.

Routines reserved for those who near their end
Are parcelled out and placed in strangers' hands.
Although those hands might be the hands of friends,
To my pride they seem just like swaddling bands
To babes. My heart is not in their commands.

A restless spirit tied to worn-out clay
And low in energy, I have no peace
And scarcely faith enough with which to pray,
As Saint Paul once did, for the blest release
That lets the soul survive, the body cease.

I cannot move nor wish the hours away
And, naked, face the longest knocks of time
That not even a game like solitaire may
Shield, a contrast from my own younger prime
When a thousand projects made the self's bright day.

Tomorrow and tomorrow I must spend
In routines different from yesterday,
Routines reserved for those who near their end.
A restless spirit tied to worn-out clay
I cannot move nor wish the hours away.

THE LONG-HEADED DOUBT

Where I grew up, neighbours were generous
And open. They did not take advantage
Of one another. There were, however,
A few who schemed to make all they could in
Any deal. Father told me who they were:
"Long-headed" was the term he used with scorn.

I watched the objects of my father's scorn
For head-length, wondering if one of us—
My self in particular—as they were
Might soon be, but from my youthful age
And inexperience I found nothing in
Cranial shape to make me know them ever.

I then tried listening and, wherever
It was possible, my mind did not scorn
To search in actions, word, motives, and in
The prejudices of those around us
For a sign or clue, a simple message
That would tell me who the long-headed were.

At last I thought I knew who of us were
Long-headed, the ones who were forever
Looking for an edge, to gain advantage
So dear to them it made them risk our scorn,
If it were known, or start a mighty fuss
That might disturb the small world we were in.

I saw long-headedness as doubt wherein
All the bonds that linked community were
Not ties but fetters; work was onerous
When done for others; and for the clever,
Sermons were butts for ridicule and scorn.
I became long-headed for advantage.

First I doubted community; with age
That doubt increased until it settled in
My secret self and made me scan with scorn
My inner motives from the days that were
Until now. Now I know doubt's an ever
Spreading virus that threatens all of us.

Wherever here in this long-headed age
Faith is found, I ask it, "Pray for us."
Prayer is the one act I no longer scorn.

MEDITATIONS ON FOOTBALL

I passed a playing field the other day
And watched a score plus two of bodies move,
Their actions patterned by a soccer ball.
It was just a game and they but bodies.
Something was needed that it did not have
And I walked off, leaving it out of sight.

But in another place and time the sight
Of a football game would have made that day
The climax of my concentration, have
Glued my eyes to every player's move,
Added body-english to whatever bodies
Imparted destination to the ball.

It's not enough to know the rules, football
Demands at least three skills from touch and sight:
Ball-control, team-work on attack, bodies
That will anticipate the coming play
On defence. Men merge in two units, move
Back and forth to give the game all they have.

But that's not enough, either. What men have
Always to conform to throughout football
Is my lord referee, watching each move
With too quick whistle and a godlike sight.
Most decisive of all's the chancy way
The ball bounces, on or off of bodies.

The game enthrals the player. His body's
In it and his mind and spirit. What have
Those who watch it on any night or day
To hear or see that makes them love football?
There, identification with a team's site
Or empathy with its struggle can move.

Since neither in my case holds, I can move
And leave the game. But do I? For bodies,
Better than minds, recall whatever site
I played in and how the team did. Muscles have
Remembered. Only to glimpse that football
Has made today a far different day.

In me today, my younger bodies move
As sight recalls games from the past I have,
Heading a no longer existent ball.

WHAT'S IN A NAME?

Men of fame and no-fame
Have asked, What's in a name?

I answer, More than chance
Or random circumstance

Names make identity
Less of a mystery.

Each name has its own ring
And when we name a thing

That name must live with it,
Make both together fit.

I hold this position
Through my intuition

In this—as in belief
In God—I've only faith.

A SPECULATION

I bear a world inside my mind
That is closer than my shadow.
It lies inside me and I know
My body's but a thin-skinned rind
Between it and the unconfined
World outside that my senses feel.
I ask two question: what is real
In either world? Is it designed?

Using symbols, I make patterns
Out of what links both worlds. They're true
In a limited sense. But what turns
My inner wheel of consciousness
And the vastness beyond my view
Is something I can only guess.

HUSBANDMAN

But he did this. From a long litany
Of things worth doing, he chose only three
And told us why he chose them when he said:
"Sow. Till. Harvest. By these the world is fed.
What better use is there for energy?"

The neighbours thought his toil mere slavery,
The payment for it only penury;
No tombstone proclaimed after he was dead:
                              "But he did this."

Those he loved recalled food was not only
Food to him; it was love's best rosary,
And when he died their simple verdict read:
"Some men's sole fame was in the words they said.
Breath was the most they gave to history,
                              but he did this."

WE HAVE AND HAVE NOT

we have and have not;
power-drunk we thirst; replete.
We are ravenous.

Only to express
self-love through love beyond self
can cure such hunger.

FORTY-FIVE YEARS OF PROGRESS

In 1949 in New Brunswick
left-wing politics was a dirty word

When I was the provincial secretary
of the C.C.F., some party members
wanted to have their letters sent
to them in plain white envelopes
the way condoms were delivered.

Now after years of social amenities
that once only the rich could afford
the social wheel has turned full circle
and left-wing politics has become
a dirty word again

This time to prevent banks and corporations
and families of wealthy individuals
from having to pay more taxes, or in many cases
having to pay taxes at all

REFORM

Reform is today
Not what it was. Now it means
Let's make the poor pay.

A FACET OF CHARITY

One morning when traffic was light in the mall
A store-owner took a little boy around his store
And whenever he saw something the boy liked, he said
"Take it, son, if it will make you glad at all."

After an hour the boy stumbled out of the store.
Weighed down with clothes he did not want very much.
He wondered if the store-owner was crazy.

But the store-owner felt like a boy-scout again
After a star-day of good things done.
The store-owner was glad.

THE GOLD

After the French of Rina Lasnier

The Incas named the gold: The Tears of God.
God wept, underneath both earth and river.
We have worn to the bone earth and river
To have these tears far from the face of God.

AN AUTOBIOGRAPHICAL INCIDENT

As a boy I had a good memory
For almost everything that I read.
And all the world of books that filled my head
Meant more than the life I saw around me.
I moved in both worlds ambidextrously
And what I thought came out in what I said.
To those who heard me, each time I talked bred
A communication difficulty.

I did not know this and I spoke my mind
In a sort of unselfconscious release
Until a classmate, far more sharp than kind,
Said what she felt in words I can't forget:
"If you only had the sense God gave geese
Maybe you might amount to something yet."

AN IRONY

After his Muse deserted him, the poet
Took offence and insulted her. The fuss
He made was rude. She listened with regret,
Then cursed him with the curse of Tantalus.

Though far finer lines than thought could evoke
Made all his dreams harbingers of renown
They always vanished soon as he awoke,
Before he had the time to write them down.

ANECDOTAL

In what we can do in life and in what
We can't, memory and forgetfulness
have their place. Throughout my adolescence
I could not stand the sight of gravy.
The very thought of it would make me sick.

Then I recalled one day in April when
A bilious brown liquid stood thick around
A manure pile in front of the cow-barn.
"What's that, daddy?" I asked my father then.
He answered me in a single word, "Gravy".

Thanks to remembering this incident,
I eat potatoes now laced with gravy
And relish that on which I once had gagged
But wonder how many phobias depend
On long forgotten misinformation

ANSWERS

I know any set
question that science answers
leads to others yet

when I saw today
rippling water and asked, "what
makes it move that way?"

I knew no one there
nor encyclopaedias could
give the full answer

MONOLOGUE

I stood and stared at you, arms akimbo;
A rage of body english shook my form
When I said, "If you want to leave me, go."

You took me at my word. The usual blow
Was not delivered, quite untrue to form.
I stood and stared at you, arms akimbo,

And watched your going, hesitant and slow,
Like the withdrawal of a wounded worm
When I said, "If you want to leave me, go."

I do not miss you very much although
I recall some good days from out the norm.
I stood and stared at you, arms akimbo

And wondered why you first became my beau.
Perhaps it was your handsome uniform.
When I said, "If you want to leave me, go."

I didn't think you'd do it. Now I know
The long dull peace without the passion-storm.
I stood and stared at you, arms akimbo,
When I said, "If you want to leave me, go."

FOURTH WALK

After the French of Victor Hugo

God! How lovely the hills with their shadow-haze!
How clear is the sky, how graceful is the sea!
What matter now the remains of fleeting days!
I touch the infinite, know eternity.

Storms! Passions! O my soul, be still in your gaze!
Never so near to God has my heart been pressed.
The West looks at me here with its eyes a-blaze,
To me the ocean speaks. I feel myself blest.

Blessed are all those who hate me or love me.
Let's concentrate on love, the spirit sublime.
Fools plough up problems or chase after glory
I wish but to live. I have so little time!

The star escapes billows where sunbeams are drowned;
The nest sings; at my feet waves roar as they roll;
In their splendour beneath me sun-rays rebound!
God! How small is mankind; how great is the soul!

All things created, bright fire, seas a-tremble,
Only half-know the most-high name of the Lord,
They utter vague sounds that only I assemble.
Each says its syllable, but I say the word.

From your voice-depths, my voice takes its starward climb!
I pray with you, mountain. I dream with you, sea!
Nature is incense, pure, eternal, sublime;
I am its incense-bearer, mild, wise, and free

HEAVEN AND HELL

After the French of Rina Lasnier

HEAVEN AND...

I draw near, Lord, I approach for living.
Again! Ah! God! Almost near enough to clutch!
My God, all that is merely perishing...
To die, Lord, having no more to do than touch.

HELL...

Rise up, Lord. From my tomb of flesh depart,
I cannot hallow you with my earthly heart.
Without my knowledge, you may in me dwell,
But if I lose you, I'll find you in my hell.

A MENTAL JOURNEY

Whatever tasks the boy did on the farm
Expressed the same feelings in him. At first,
Curiosity prompted by the question
"Can I do it?" And with its answer, pride.
As muscles tired, pride waned. But with work done
Weariness gave way to relaxed content.

And this process, whatever its content,
Was not, he saw, tied to chores on the farm
But pervaded all that is ever done.
What starts with some uncertainty at first
Soon quickens to the headlong pace of pride
Over-riding weariness and question

To find its end in rest. Now the question
Left him then was what to choose for content.
Skill by itself was not enough for pride
—A case in point was chores upon the farm—
Work that seemed too arduous at first
Became too easy by repetition.

But "hard" or "easy", after work was done,
Then led him on to a greater question,
One quite beyond his provenance at first
When with his parents' wishes he'd been content.
After he had outgrown them and the farm
What could he find with which to feed his pride?

He found the world a maze of pomp and pride
Where everything that is ever done
Finds somewhere justification. The farm
Had asked and answered just a simple question,
But a company and a government
Offered riddles for his mind from the first.

In a dream the answer came: "*You must first
Hunt out right words to link your being's pride
To all your being's wordless part. Content
Is not for you, whose task is never done.
But it will free you from any question
And from the logic of your father's farm.*"

PSYCHO-SOMATIC

Skin saves the body
from all the outer chaos:
words are the mind's skin.

THE CRICKET

Across the floor the cricket crawled.
I watched its progress, then I said:
"This creature is as good as dead.
There is no procramme in its head
To fit the place where now it's walled."

Later that night I heard a song
Well up from underneath a chair,
Breaking the stillness black and bare.
The full duet discovered there
Told me just why my words were wrong.

TO AN OLD BIRD

You want to fly back
to live in your nestling days.
But where are your wings?

ON DISPLAY

After the French of Leconte de Lisle

Like a sad beast, battered, down where the dark dust swirls,
Neck in a chain, howling to the sun's summer hood,
Let who wishes   display his heart stained with its blood
Upon your shameless pavement, man-eating churls.

To put a sterile flame into your vacant eye,
To importune laughter or a vulgar distress,
Tear off, if you must, the light radiant dress
That hallows your pleasure and divine modesty.

In my mute pride, in my tomb where no fame can be,
Must I be engulfed for a bleak eternity?
I shall not sell you my ecstasy and rage.

I shall not give my life to your derisive hoots,
I shall not do a dance upon your banal stage
Together with your mountebanks and prostitutes.

LOVE-POET

Lost in passion's element
full fifty poems he spun
When 'twere better he had spent
that time in writing one.

DON'T TAKE ME OVER

Don't take me over with a love full-blown
Exerting the whole weight of all your will.
Give me a space that I can call my own

In which this self has room to grow alone
The one true form that it was meant to fill.
Don't take me over with a love full-blown,

But when all the best that I am has grown
Its shape, then join yourself to me and fill.
Give me a shape that I can call my own

Whose place is not a footstool nor a throne
But a clear window and a windowsill.
Don't take me over with a love full-blown

But let two lives of equal strength make one
Bright landscape that knows neither vale nor hill.
Give me a space that I can call my own

And each shall meet as equal not as clone.
In this way we'll share passion's utmost thrill.
Don't take me over with a love full-blown.
Give me a space that I can call my own.

BARRIERS

I tried to tame the world outside my skin
That seemed too big and wild a place for me.
My efforts were as if they had not been;

They put out barriers, small enough and thin
To reflect my own personality.
I tried to tame the world outside my skin

Transplanting seeds, home grown, from my within
To give the world the dream I hoped to be.
My efforts were as if they had not been.

The struggle then was too one-sided, mean;
My seedlings died in life's immensity.
I tried to tame the world outside my skin

But, wiser now, I am aware that skin
And I are false illusions, sophistry.
My efforts were as if they had not been.

Like Don Quixote, who only lived to spin
The windmills of impossibility
I tried to tame the world outside my skin.
My efforts were as if they had not been.

PIGEONS

On the beams in the barn the whole day through
From early spring till mating time was over
The gentle pigeons used to bill and coo.

The sunbeams that chinks in the barn walls drew
Floated down the dust of last year's clover
On the beams of the barn the whole day through.

No change there. Nothing was old, nothing new.
Inside the silence over and over
The gentle pigeons used to bill and coo,

With beaks and heads together, two by two.
Lover doted on nothing but lover
On the beams in the barn the whole day through.

Gone are the years when the barn was new,
The hay-mow's beams, the snug roof over.
The gentle pigeons used to bill and coo,

But now they're gone. I don't know where they flew.
Still mind holds fast to what no eyes recover;
On the beams in the barn the whole day through
The gentle pigeons used to bill and coo.

ON KEATS' "Ode on a Grecian Urn"

To me, "Ode on a Grecian Urn" is Keats'
Greatest failure. A false logic here is his.
His great "Beauty and Truth" assumption cheats,
Confounding what ought to be with what is.

Of course, Beauty can be found in Truth. None
Deny that Truth is Beauty. But Truth's Beauty
And Beauty's Truth are not the same. The one
Delights in *is*, the other in *should be*.

I think that his too facile confusion
Persuaded Keats to draw this conclusion:
"That's all you know and all you need to know".

Such words can only work in Elysium,
A magic place where too few mortals come
And only urns and mad young poets go.

AT THE GRAVE-YARD

I can't see her stone
without tears as I think of
all the good years gone ...

FOOT-DRILL

They'd be marching yet
Had not the platoon-leader
Ordered them to halt.

BUCK JONES

Of all the boys at school my hero was
Buck Jones. There was only one reason why:
Whatever happened from whatever cause
Nothing done to him ever made him cry.

Making light of a real bad ankle-sprain
He'd play at basketball without a limp.
When the teacher's strap swung with might and main
His calm control made teacher seem a wimp.

I've seen him—when he had impetigo
On his wrist—add to that pain one pain more.
He'd squeeze the scabs to make the green pus flow
And pour formaldehyde into each sore.

The only time I ever saw him crack
Was when we watched a car break his dog's back.

AN EPIGRAM

Though deeds may cause biography
Words I write are the best of me.

NOW IT IS A COLD DECEMBER

Now it is a cold December.
There's friction in our loves' mind-set:
All the things I best remember
Are those I hoped you would forget.

LAZARUS

After the French of Rina Lasnier

He said to me: "Come, take my place in death!"
He cried over me the cry of incarnation,
He changed the face and fortune of my path,
He crucified me on the cross of resurrection.

THE DEAD

I

In the grave-yard under the grass
Nothing is left of the dead, gone
And buried beneath a green lawn,
Except their bones, and these will pass
As time's great jaws, stronger than brass,
Will swallow them, and in the place
Of their vanishing leave no trace
By which to remember what was.

Though no one will know who they were
Who once drew in the sun-warmed air
With human lungs and moved live bones,
Merely their having been will be
A timeless fact, transcending stones.
All that's gone is identity.

II

There is no destruction there.
In any world there's only change.
All that ever was in the range
Of being still exists somewhere .
In some shape, and it will fare,
Many-formed, inside being's range
Where mass and motion interchange
And all things their full valence bear.

Our thoughts are tied to but one space
And time, dependent on a heart
That learns to fear the passing days.
Though scattered far the dead are free
From fear their selves may come apart;
They are more alive now than we.

SUN-LOVER'S DIRECTIONS

Put me in a shallow grave when life's done
Where sun-soaked soil may warm my bones' cold night,
And should a miracle restore life's light
I want my head to face the morning sun.

DUST

Earth's dark with dust. In sky the sun
Holds light and warmth in its presence,
And yet we know when each day's done
Dust can fuel incandescence.

May gathered dust from all my years
Kindle a deep rose in my twilight
As—ubiquitous as prayers—
Its thick motes burn from dark to bright

NO MORE I TRUST

No more I trust my mind's reality
Although the shaping years have come and gone
I'm the bond-slave of association
And know how much they have mis-shapened me.

Their limits weigh on what I hear and see,
The songs I listen to, the books I read;
The same applies to any sense I heed.
How can I reach a world that's ego-free?

I would lie, eyes closed, alone, oh so still
Till I lost my self in the miracle
Of a new-awakened and fresh rebirth,
Absorbed for the first time in the motion
And shine of a grand unfettered ocean
And the natural sounds of mindless earth.

IN US OUR FEARS AND LONGINGS WAR

In us our fears and longings war.
We do not wish to be alone
Yet dread to face the things unknown
We sense in other people are;
Therefore our selves we won't unbar.
Although our egos ache to touch,
Such contact with another's clutch
Might somehow on us leave a scar.

But around us everywhere, dark,
Light, earth, sky in all their powers
Unleash their energies and spark
The myriad forms the world assumes
Where motion's but a change of rooms
And aeons count no more than hours.

LIFE-LOVERS

When in our youthful joys our arms we fling
And easy breathe the unresistant air,
Our lungs draw in our body's mindless prayer:
How sweet the debt we owe for early Spring.

When we are old and feel our joints' sharp rage
We do not doubt their motions' worth the pain
And heaving lungs still offer thanks again:
How sweet to be alive at any age.

A RESPONSE TO CRITICISM

Of my poems one reviewer wrote, given
Seven books to review:
He's the seventh one; no seventh heaven
Here. These will never do.

Saturday's child must work for a living.
I found his words murder
As I read them with more than misgiving.
They made me work harder.

THE TROUBLE WITH LIGHT

... after the after-glow
we live with the shadow.